TED SPEED OFF

Written by Shannen Yauger

Illustrated by Vanessa Toye

© 2024 The Good and the Beautiful, LLC
goodandbeautiful.com

TED AND TOM
and the
FAST
CAR

Ted and Tom
find a big box.

"What can we make?" asks Ted.

They get a lot of stuff.
Dad helps the boys.

"We will be back,"
Ted says.

"See you soon," Tom says
as he hugs Dad.

Ted and Tom
are in a fast car.

ZOOM!

Ted and Tom zoom past the red car.

They zip past the blue car.

The red car and the
blue car zoom past
Ted and Tom.

"Go, Ted! Go fast!" Tom says.

Ted and Tom zip this way.

They zoom that way.

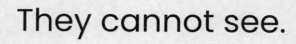

They cannot see.

"There is so much dirt," Ted says.

"Go that way!" Tom says.

Ted zips past the blue car.

"Go this way!"

20

"Go this way!"

Ted zooms past the red car.

"Go, Ted, go!" yells Tom.

The boys cross the line.

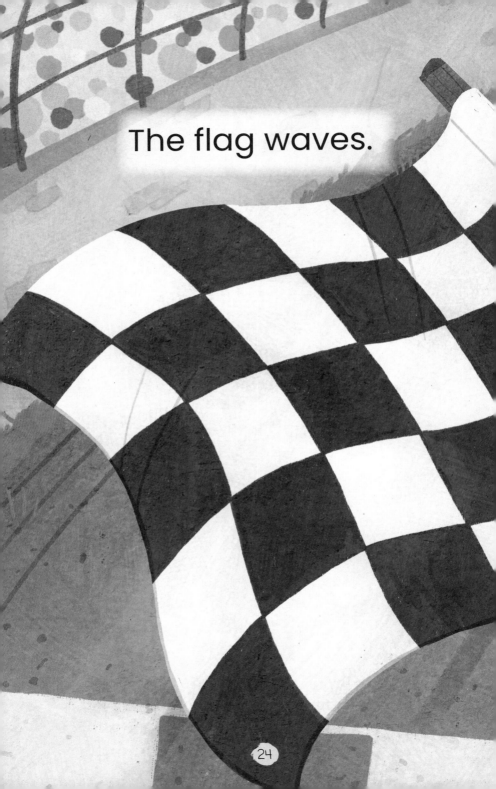

The flag waves.

Ted and Tom win!

The man in the blue car
jumps up and down.

Ted and Tom wave and
drive off.

At last they make it home.

Dad is glad to have the boys back safe and sound.

TED AND TOM

Take a

TRAIN

Ted and Tom
find a big box.

"What can we make?"
asks Ted.

They get a lot of stuff. Mom helps the boys.

"We will be back," Ted says to Mom.

"See you soon!" Tom yells.

TOOT, TOOT!

"Look at that train, Tom," says Ted.

"Can we go that fast?"
Tom asks Ted.

"Let's go!" says Tom.

They speed past the fast
train.

They speed around
the hill.

They speed in the cave.

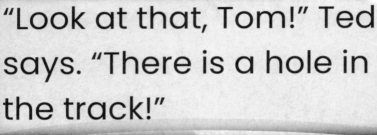

"Look at that, Tom!" Ted says. "There is a hole in the track!"

Ted and Tom slow down.

"We must stop that train!" Tom says.

They go back on the track.

They go back
in the cave.

The train is
by the hill.

"Stop, stop!"
Ted and
Tom yell.

They wave at the
man on the train.

The man does not
see them.

The train goes
into the cave.

Ted and Tom go by the man on the train.

"Stop, stop!" they yell.

The man on the train sees Ted and Tom.

He stops the train just in time.

He waves to Ted
and Tom.

They saved
the train!

At last they make it home.

Mom is glad to have the boys back safe and sound.